Piano • Vocal • Guitar

NEW STANDARDS

ISBN 0-7935-9284-4

HAL•LEONARD®
CORPORATION

7777 W. BLUEMOUND RD. P.O. BOX 13819 MILWAUKEE, WI 53213

Visit Hal Leonard Online at
www.halleonard.com

ALL I ASK OF YOU

from THE PHANTOM OF THE OPERA

Music by ANDREW LLOYD WEBBER
Lyrics by CHARLES HART
Additional Lyrics by RICHARD STILGOE

Andante

RAOUL: No more talk of dark-ness, for-get these wide-eyed fears; I'm

here, noth-ing can harm you, my words will warm and calm you.

Let me be your free-dom, let day-light dry your tears; I'm

BEAUTY AND THE BEAST

from Walt Disney's BEAUTY AND THE BEAST

Lyrics by HOWARD ASHMAN
Music by ALAN MENKEN

AMERICAN PIE

Words and Music by
DON McLEAN

MCA Music Publishing

Moderately

So bye - bye, Miss A - mer - i - can Pie__ Drove my

Chev - y to the lev - ee but the lev - ee was dry.__ Them

good ole boys __ were drink - in' whis - key and rye__ Sing - in'

To Coda

this - 'll be the day __ that I __ die,

This - 'll be the day __ that I __ die. _____

1. Did you __ write the book of love __ and do you __
2.-4. *See additional lyrics*

__ have faith in God a - bove?_ If the Bi - ble tells __

__ you so __ Now do you __ be - lieve __ in

Additional Lyrics

2. Now for ten years we've been on our own,
   And moss grows fat on a rollin' stone
   But that's not how it used to be
   When the jester sang for the king and queen
   In a coat he borrowed from James Dean
   And a voice that came from you and me
   Oh and while the king was looking down,
   The jester stole his thorny crown
   The courtroom was adjourned,
   No verdict was returned
   And while Lenin read a book on Marx
   The quartet practiced in the park
   And we sang dirges in the dark
   The day the music died
   We were singin'... bye-bye... etc.

3. Helter-skelter in the summer swelter
   The birds flew off with a fallout shelter
   Eight miles high and fallin' fast,
   it landed foul on the grass
   The players tried for a forward pass,
   With the jester on the sidelines in a cast
   Now the half-time air was sweet perfume
   While the sergeants played a marching tune
   We all got up to dance
   But we never got the chance
   'Cause the players tried to take the field,
   The marching band refused to yield
   Do you recall what was revealed
   The day the music died
   We started singin'... bye-bye... etc.

4. And there we were all in one place,
   A generation lost in space
   With no time left to start again
   So come on, Jack be nimble, Jack be quick,
   Jack Flash sat on a candlestick
   'Cause fire is the devil's only friend
   And as I watched him on the stage
   My hands were clenched in fists of rage
   No angel born in hell
   Could break that Satan's spell
   And as the flames climbed high into the night
   To light the sacrificial rite
   I saw Satan laughing with delight
   The day the music died
   He was singin'... bye-bye... etc.

Can You Feel The Love Tonight

(as performed by ELTON JOHN)

from Walt Disney Pictures' THE LION KING

Music by ELTON JOHN
Lyrics by TIM RICE

CAN'T HELP FALLING IN LOVE

from BLUE HAWAII

Words and Music by GEORGE DAVID WEISS,
HUGO PERETTI and LUIGI CREATORE

CANDLE IN THE WIND

Music by ELTON JOHN
Words by BERNIE TAUPIN

Good-bye Nor - ma Jean, _____ though I nev - er
Lone - li - ness _____ was tough, _____ the tough-est role

knew you _____ at all you had the grace to hold your-self _____ while
you ev - er played. Hol - ly-wood cre - at - ed a su - per-star _____ and

those a - round _ you crawled. _____ They crawled out of the
pain was the price you paid. _____ E - ven when you

CHANGE THE WORLD

featured on the Motion Picture Soundtrack PHENOMENON

Words and Music by GORDON KENNEDY,
TOMMY SIMS and WAYNE KIRKPATRICK

CHARIOTS OF FIRE

Music by
VANGELIS

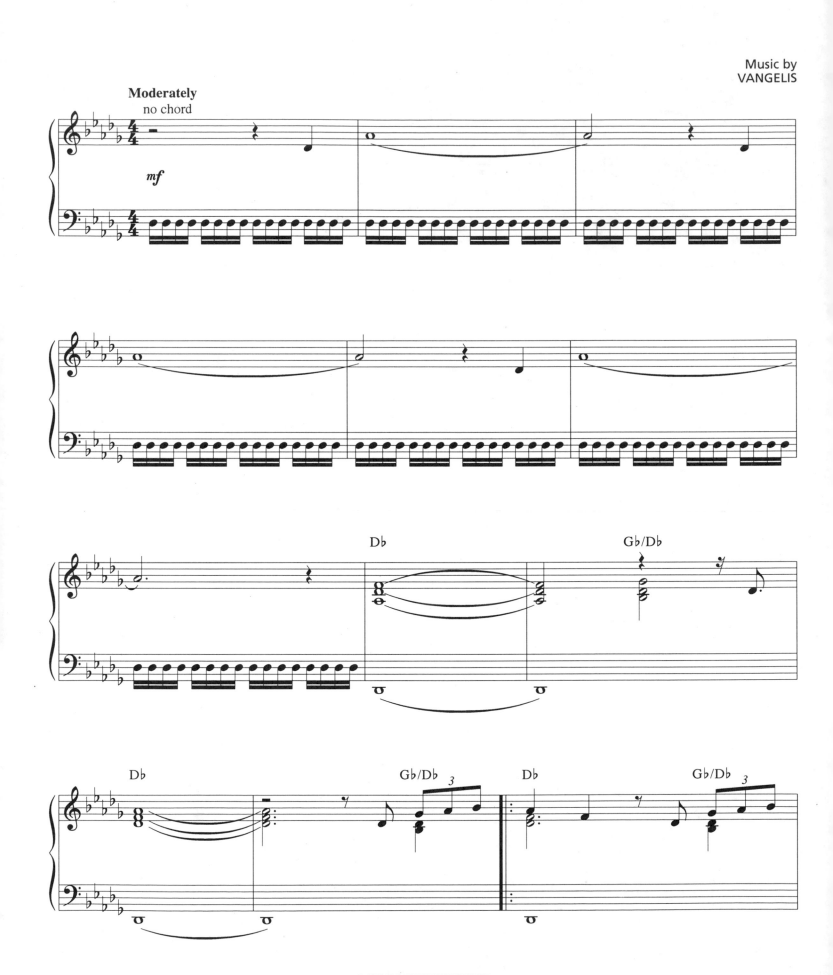

COLORS OF THE WIND

from Walt Disney's POCAHONTAS

Music by ALAN MENKEN
Lyrics by STEPHEN SCHWARTZ

DUST IN THE WIND

Words and Music by
KERRY LIVGREN

Repeat and Fade

ENDLESS LOVE

Words and Music by
LIONEL RICHIE

EVERY BREATH YOU TAKE

Written and Composed by
STING

HAVE I TOLD YOU LATELY

Words and Music by
VAN MORRISON

Have I told ___ you late-ly that I love you? Have I

told you there's no one else __ a-bove __ you?

Fill my heart __ with glad - ness, take a-way all __ my sad - ness,

ease my trou-bles that's___ what you do.

1. For the
2. *Instrumental*

morn - in' sun in all___ it's glo - ry greets the

day with hope and com-fort, too.___

You fill my life with laugh - ter and some-how you make it bet - ter,

FORREST GUMP - MAIN TITLE
(Feather Theme)
from the Paramount Motion Picture FORREST GUMP

Music by
ALAN SILVESTRI

HERO

Words and Music by MARIAH CAREY
and WALTER AFANASIEFF

Moderately

E(add9)   B/D#   C#m7   E/B   A   E/G#

F#m7   B9sus   B   E(add9)   D6/9

There's a he - ro if you look in - side__ your heart. You don't
long__ road when you face the world__ a - lone. No one

C#m7   B9sus   B

have to be__ a-fraid of what you are._____ There's an an-
reach - es out__ a hand for you to hold._____ You can find__

E(add9)   D/F#

- swer if you reach in - to__ your soul_____ and the
__ love if you search with - in__ your-self_____ and the

IF WE HOLD ON TOGETHER

from THE LAND BEFORE TIME

Words and Music by JAMES HORNER
and WILL JENNINGS

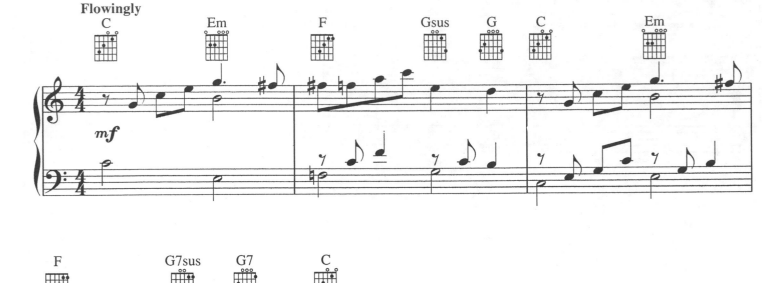

Don't lose your way with each pass-ing day.
Souls in the wind must learn how to bend,

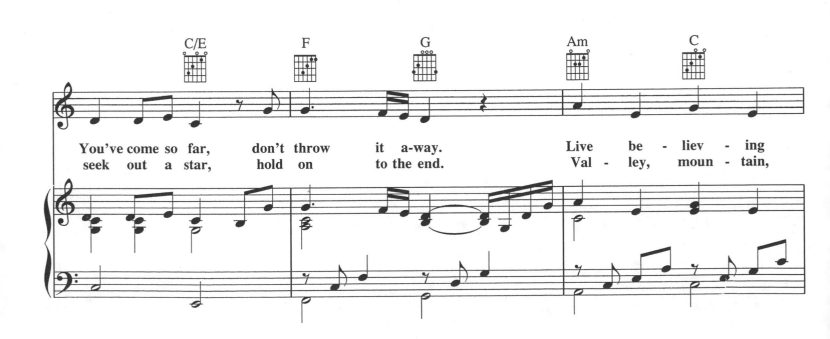

You've come so far, don't throw it a-way.
seek out a star, hold on to the end.

Live be-liev-ing
Val-ley, moun-tain,

IMAGINE

Words and Music by
JOHN LENNON

IT'S ALL COMING BACK TO ME NOW

Words and Music by
JIM STEINMAN

Moderately, with feeling

There were nights when the wind _ was so cold _ that my bod-y froze in bed if I just lis-tened to it right out-side the win-dow.

There were days when the sun _ was so cruel, _ all the

THE KEEPER OF THE STARS

Words and Music by KAREN STALEY,
DANNY MAYO and DICKEY LEE

LET IT BE

Words and Music by JOHN LENNON
and PAUL McCARTNEY

When I find my-self in times of trou-ble

Instrumental

Moth-er Mar-y comes to me Speak-ing words of wis-dom, Let it

be and in my hour of dark-ness She is

MEMORY
from CATS

Music by ANDREW LLOYD WEBBER
Text by TREVOR NUNN after T.S. ELIOT

Freely ♩.=50

GRIZABELLA

Mid - night._____ Not a sound from the pave - ment._____ Has the moon lost her
Me - mory_____ all a - lone in the moon - light_____ I can smile at the

me - mory?_____ She is smil - ing a - lone._____ In the
old days,_____ I was beau - ti - ful then._____ I re -

MOON RIVER

from the Paramount Picture BREAKFAST AT TIFFANY'S

Words by JOHNNY MERCER
Music by HENRY MANCINI

PIANO MAN

Words and Music
by BILLY JOEL

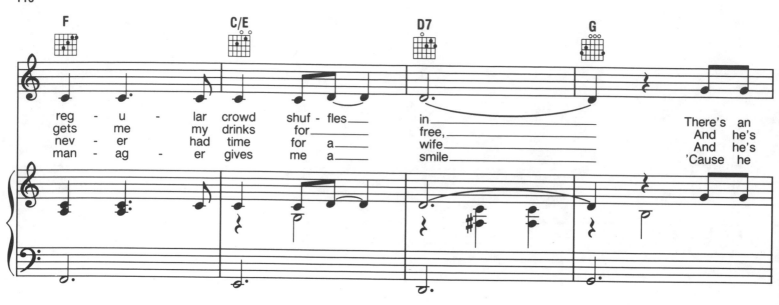

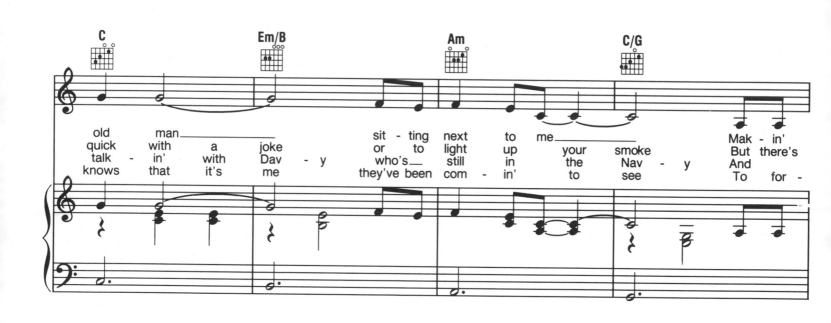

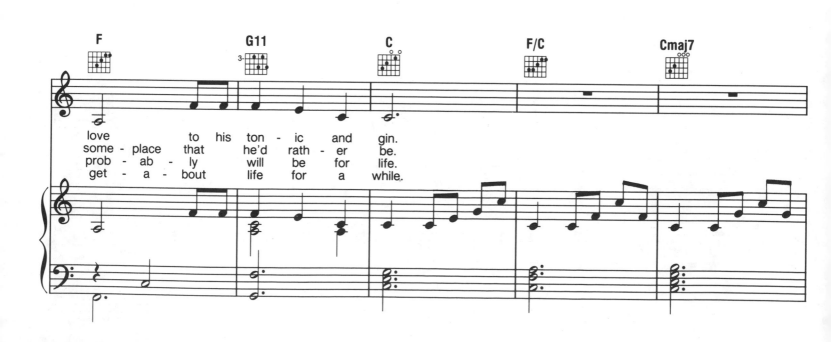

I wore a young - er man's clothes." _____
I could get out of this place." _____
bet - ter than drink - in' a - lone." _____
"Man what are you do -in' here?" _____

Da da da _____
Da da da _____
Instrumental _____
Da da da _____

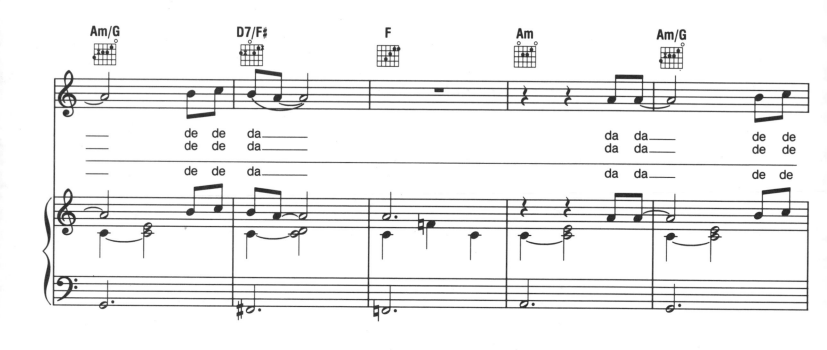

_____ de de da _____
_____ de de da _____
_____ de de da _____

da da _____ de de
da da _____ de de
da da _____ de de

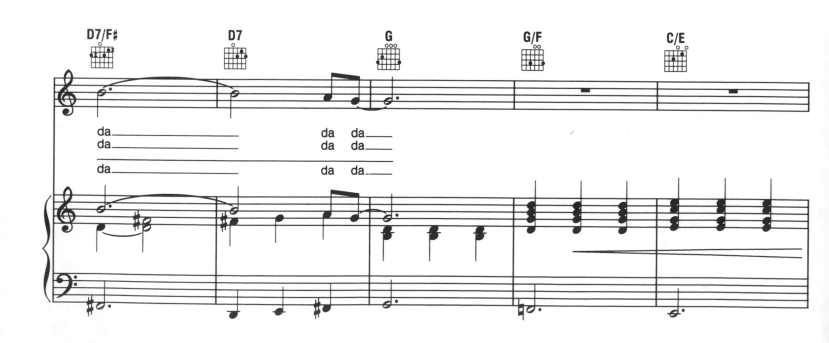

da _____ da da _____
da _____ da da _____
da _____ da da _____

THE POWER OF LOVE

Words by MARY SUSAN APPLEGATE and JENNIFER RUSH
Music by CANDY DEROUGE and GUNTHER MENDE

THE RAINBOW CONNECTION
from THE MUPPET MOVIE

By PAUL WILLIAMS
and KENNETH L. ASCHER

SOMEWHERE OUT THERE
from AN AMERICAN TAIL

Words and Music by JAMES HORNER,
BARRY MANN and CYNTHIA WEIL

Some - where___ out there be - neath the pale moon - light___ some - one's think - in' of me and

MCA Music Publishing

through, then we'll be to - geth - er some-where out there, out

where dreams come true.

Save the Best for Last

Words and Music by PHIL GALDSTON,
JON LIND and WENDY WALDMAN

STAND BY ME

Words and Music by BEN E. KING,
JERRY LEIBER and MIKE STOLLER

TEARS IN HEAVEN

Words and Music by ERIC CLAPTON
and WILL JENNINGS

UNCHAINED MELODY

featured in the Motion Picture GHOST

Lyric by HY ZARET
Music by ALEX NORTH

A WHOLE NEW WORLD
(Aladdin's Theme)
from Walt Disney's ALADDIN

Music by ALAN MENKEN
Lyrics by TIM RICE

WHAT A WONDERFUL WORLD

featured in the Motion Picture GOOD MORNING VIETNAM

Words and Music by GEORGE DAVID WEISS
and BOB THIELE

WHEN I FALL IN LOVE

featured in the TriStar Motion Picture SLEEPLESS IN SEATTLE

Words by EDWARD HEYMAN
Music by VICTOR YOUNG

YESTERDAY

Words and Music by JOHN LENNON
and PAUL McCARTNEY

Moderately, with expression

Yes-ter- day,___ all my trou-bles seemed so
Sud-den- ly,___ I'm not half the man___ I

far a- way,___ Now it looks as though___ they're
used to be, There's a sha- dow hang- ing

YOU'VE GOT A FRIEND

Words and Music by
CAROLE KING

Contemporary Classics

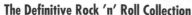

Your favorite songs for piano, voice and guitar.

The Definitive Rock 'n' Roll Collection

A classic collection of the best songs from the early rock 'n' roll years – 1955-1966. 97 songs, including: Barbara Ann • Chantilly Lace • Dream Lover • Duke Of Earl • Earth Angel • Great Balls Of Fire • Louie, Louie • Rock Around The Clock • Ruby Baby • Runaway • (Seven Little Girls) Sitting In The Back Seat • Stay • Surfin' U.S.A. • Wild Thing • Woolly Bully • and more.
00490195 ....$27.95

The Big Book Of Rock

78 of rock's biggest hits, including: Addicted To Love • American Pie • Born To Be Wild • Cold As Ice • Dust In The Wind • Free Bird • Goodbye Yellow Brick Road • Groovin' • Hey Jude • I Love Rock N Roll • Lay Down Sally • Layla • Livin' On A Prayer • Louie Louie • Maggie May • Me And Bobby McGee • Monday, Monday • Owner Of A Lonely Heart • Shout • Walk This Way • We Didn't Start The Fire • You Really Got Me • and more.
00311566...$19.95

Big Book Of Movie And TV Themes

Over 90 familiar themes, including: Alfred Hitchcock Theme • Beauty And The Beast • Candle On The Water • Theme From *E.T.* • Endless Love • Hawaii Five-O • I Love Lucy • Theme From *Jaws* • Jetsons • Major Dad Theme • The Masterpiece • Mickey Mouse March • The Munsters Theme • Theme From *Murder, She Wrote* • Mystery • Somewhere Out There • Unchained Melody • Won't You Be My Neighbor • and more!
00311582 ....$19.95

The Best Rock Songs Ever

70 of the best rock songs from yesterday and today, including: All Day And All Of The Night • All Shook Up • Ballroom Blitz • Bennie And The Jets • Blue Suede Shoes • Born To Be Wild • Boys Are Back In Town • Every Breath You Take • Faith • Free Bird • Hey Jude • I Still Haven't Found What I'm Looking For • Livin' On A Prayer • Lola • Louie Louie • Maggie May • Money • (She's) Some Kind Of Wonderful • Takin' Care Of Business • Walk This Way • We Didn't Start The Fire • We Got The Beat • Wild Thing • more!
00490424 ....$16.95

The Best Of 90s Rock

30 songs, including: Alive • I'd Do Anything For Love (But I Won't Do That) • Livin' On The Edge • Losing My Religion • Two Princes • Walking On Broken Glass • Wind Of Change • and more.
00311668 ....$14.95

35 Classic Hits

35 contemporary favorites, including: Beauty And The Beast • Dust In The Wind • Just The Way You Are • Moon River • The River Of Dreams • Somewhere Out There • Tears In Heaven • When I Fall In Love • A Whole New World (Aladdin's Theme) • and more.
00311654 ....$12.95

55 Contemporary Standards

55 favorites, including: Alfie • Beauty And The Beast • Can't Help Falling In Love • Candle In The Wind • Have I Told You Lately • How Am I Supposed To Live Without You • Memory • The River Of Dreams • Sea Of Love • Tears In Heaven • Up Where We Belong • When I Fall In Love • and more.
00311670...$15.95

Women of Modern Rock

25 songs from contemporary chanteuses, including: As I Lay Me Down • Connection • Feed The Tree • Galileo • Here And Now • Look What Love Has Done • Love Sneakin' Up On You • Walking On Broken Glass • You Oughta Know • Zombie • and more.
00310093 ....$14.95

Jock Rock Hits

32 stadium-shaking favorites, including: Another One Bites The Dust • The Boys Are Back In Town • Freeze-Frame • Gonna Make You Sweat (Everybody Dance Now) • I Got You (I Feel Good) • Na Na Hey Hey Kiss Him Goodbye • Rock & Roll – Part II (The Hey Song) • Shout • Tequila • We Are The Champions • We Will Rock You • Whoomp! (There It Is) • Wild Thing • and more.
00310105...$14.95

Rock Ballads

31 sentimental favorites, including: All For Love • Bed Of Roses • Dust In The Wind • Everybody Hurts • Right Here Waiting • Tears In Heaven • and more.
00311673 ....$14.95

0997